THE HARPER

THE HARPER

Peter Redgrove

CAPE POETRY

Published by Jonathan Cape 2006

2 4 6 8 10 9 7 5 3 1

Copyright © the Estate of Peter Redgrove 2006

Peter Redgrove has asserted his right under the Copyright, Designs
and Patents Act 1988 to be identified as the author of this work

First published in Great Britain in 2006 by
Jonathan Cape
Random House, 20 Vauxhall Bridge Road, London SW1V 2SA

Random House Australia (Pty) Limited
20 Alfred Street, Milsons Point, Sydney,
New South Wales 2061, Australia

Random House New Zealand Limited
18 Poland Road, Glenfield,
Auckland 10, New Zealand

Random House South Africa (Pty) Limited
Isle of Houghton, Corner of Boundary Road & Carse O'Gowrie,
Houghton 2198, South Africa

The Random House Group Limited Reg. No. 954009
www.randomhouse.co.uk

A CIP catalogue record for this book is
available from the British Library

ISBN 9780224077934 (from January 2007)
ISBN 0224077937

Typeset in Bembo by Palimpsest Book Production Limited, Polmont, Stirlingshire
Printed and bound in Great Britain by William Clowes Ltd, Beccles, Suffolk

CONTENTS

ACKNOWLEDGEMENTS

Acknowledgements are due to the editors of the following:

Boxkite, Manhattan Review, Metre, Poetry Cornwall, Poetry London, Poetry Review, Poetry Wales, Stand, The Times Literary Supplement

Thanks are due to the Royal Literary Fund for their financial support during the writing of these poems.

SONAR

The sonar of spring thunder,
        hollow boxes shoved across a stage,
                the percussionist's kit
Moved across the hills;
        facing north, so the weather
                emerges from his left,
Thunder makes the noises
        of torn wood, or of wood
                thundering with wet leaves
In the gust, wood carved into
        sonar boxes, new percussions,
                wooden bells and church organs;
The pre-storm sunshine,
        the consonance between women
                in the rain and trees
In the rain, the thundering skirts,
        the thunder-gowning of a gateway,
                women chatting
Under a rainy tree
        in the enormous
                valley-echo after thunder:
A trough after the thunder-peak
        and a valley-echo of silence.

SPIDEROUS LIZARD

The breakers pumping fine spray
                into the cliff air like spinnerets
                                creating cinemas of mist.
Gates, trees and a long wall.
                Not milking
                                but silking the spider
Called the Silver Weaver.
                A Lizard spider on a warm rock:
                        seven different silks
From seven different glands,
                bullet-proof spidersilk.
                        Moments of silk.
The Lizard,
                all restored and in place there,
                      a silver tree that led us
To a stone well; a whitebeam
                turning silver in the breeze
                      as though it were filling with water;
Rolled into silver as though
                the contents of the well
                      were a tree spinning silk.
Two gulls,
                flying across the cliff-face,
                      shifted its immense gaze.

BALL LIGHTNING

A waterfall in a vaporous glade,
        Ladders of vapour
                propped against the apple-trees
Everywhere.
        The devotion in the old dog's face
            as he gazes round and round
His mistress's garden.
        The pleasant, salt-silvered
            old house.
The loaf on the slate shelf,
        the patient ferment.
                An agate ball of lightning floats
Out of the charged orchard
        like an apple-ghost
            offering itself in turn
To our lips: house,
        dog, lover, woman,
            out of the girdle of trees
Shedding their windfalls
        in shining cascades like waterfalls;
            she got a look from it
That now she wears
        random and swamping,
            and so do I
In the smell of apple-mortality
        which is sweet,
               there are tears like windfalls
Dried on our cheeks;
        this apple-mush, these tears
           the real home of all,
Fruit, dog, woman, lover,
        ceaseless waterfall and ancient house,
           vaporous stairs that
Wait for our ascending.

SCENT-EVENT

She takes passage through the grain
            of the sky's electricities.
                        Electric cities.
There is an outer room of stone
            and an inner room of foliage
                        like an outward tomb
Burst with inner trees.
            The somas distilled
                        by the ten bones of the head
Are bright, pleasing, lovely;
            the laboratory of the mouth
                        with its nine retorts
Distils bright and innocent saliva,
            dew for her mouth.
                        She looks relaxed
Holding a glass of water and sipping from it
            or holding a glass retort.
                        There is food in sleep.
The demonic tension in the sky
            means the master-perfume of the world
                        is forming.
Still lingering in her sheets
            this perfume that is in her sleep
                        is dynamic,
The sheets are white
            as speeding water. She dreams
                        of an exhausted skull
Which rolls out into the sunlight,
            very gently its bones begin to ease
                        like the valves of a pine-cone
In the warm patch of sunlight
            (And a pineal smell expands the forest.)

And I cannot of course
      see these dreams
            but I can smell
Their individual stories
      in this unfolding
            scent–event.

BLACK VIRGINS

In that state when
       the rooms are radiant,
              the virgin groom consumes
New bread with his bride,
       and wine
              vivid as hymeneal blood.
She throws back her snowy veil
       to feed, the woman
              of ebony, ivory, and musk . . .
The baby of their union
       fingers the mother-button
            found feeding,
Garments part like cobwebs spun
       by the fugitive buttons,
              light twists off and on
In the discs of motherpearl
       like a lighthouse
              swinging its tall beam
As into a sea
       of milky sleep he sinks,
            black child
Into a seethe of white.

IN THE ESPLUMEOR

A residence in the moon
             after death, the thin clear vessel
                          lying on its back,
The church full of dreams
             like an aethyr,
                          that is the cathedral
With the million simultaneous altars
             where the dreams cross,
                          that is the body
Of Goddess with its nave,
             dreaming which is awakening
                          in her service.
The serpent corrupts in its vaulted bottle,
             the product is living gold,
                          but water, sap, milk, blood,
Semen, potable gold, represent
             but different states
                          of the one elixir
Whose vessel is the entire
             cycle of the moon, and yourself
                          lying here with me
On earth. In Ancient Greece
             Hero equals Ghost,
                          one who has made the crossing,
Gone to Goddess, and in the dawn
             travelled off in the cathedral, elsewhere.
The radical moisture at the fork
             of the body shining with its sweat
                          of love is
The sidereal balsam of the five-pointed star
             called Nimue,
                          it is a fat of manna

And a witch's butter
        called Madew,
                and a ray or radiation
Of a personal star above,
        for it is said
                the living and the dead
Have each a star, even its outscouring
        cast on earth is
                a springtime condition.
The blessed waters blend
        in the laboratorium above
                to descend and wake the dead,
Rousing them out of their sleep, maybe as
        the exaltations of the nettles
                which burn too
And the colour of the day shines
        and sparkles in the stardew of the nettlebeds
                of medicinable poison.

SHE INDOORS

There thou art a crowned queen resting
            over the fountain as known to thee;
                        passing from room to room, adjusting
The distilling magnetisms,
            foliage that cannot be seen but whispers,
                        foliage that flows
In cool electrical breezes;
            a kiss swoops
                        out of the blouse white as bone,
A bottle of magnetism
            which has been left open,
                        the home built
As clothes are cut, to guide
            such radiations along passages; the bed
                        a furnace of soft peaches.
She enters the living room
            as if she were a vapour,
                        or a ghost-yacht
White-sailed
            and smelling of summer fields
                        and when such elixirs
Find a surface to spread upon, they enlarge
            in munificent rainbows . . .
                        but generally
Our movements send out a spring smell
            of electricals, of kitchen radium:
                        what an electrical dresser she is!
What plunging alembic-necks, what
            magnetic necklaces! or under
                        the rose-roof of the shower, or by

The peacock of the cooker, the multitude
              wearing those fine-day dresses of the dry air
                          which crackle
And like peacocks or silks shriek.

SORCERESS IN MAUVE

Who loves getting dirty
    and loves standing
        drenched in the rain
Since this
    enables her to prophesy.
        She is a pacy spicy chick
And bowses
    over his body-everything
        with her every-thought.
She enters the penetralia
    of the most ordinary room,
        being inwardly
Satisfied with mere space, enters
    the vaults of the ancient book
        ample as a forest of leaves;
Then she sleeps and ages
    a hundred years; wakes
        in her youth, renewed.
She can come out in the form
    of other people's wizards;
        at one time they all tried to
Prevent her being a wizard
    on the grounds that she was a girl.
        She wears diamonds and furs
Like the World's Vagina; out of the neck
    of the spacious garment an
        ejaculation soft as air.
Her perfume fills the potential sky
    at midnight, like hair shaken out,
        the hair that protects her
With its wings folded
    about her head, and there is
        in her urine
A secret garden.

CORNISH PERSEPHONE

The little Christmas tree asserts
        its pagan presence
                aglow with electric bulbs
In the shapes of flowers, dew, castles, St Nicolas,
        all of them bursting light from within;
                then, suddenly it takes hold
And becomes a person;
        the pine-perfume lovingly reaches
                out of it, soaking up
A tincture of radiation
        from the small light-engines.
                It is as though
The fairy on the peak,
        the star welding at the tip of her wand,
                has created the foliage
By rolling her green dress down,
        and stands there,
                with the tree her whole garment,
Gifts about her feet,
        the star fissioning on her wand,
                visiting us
In a green shape at the steep year's end:
        the Giantess in her lair,
                the Cornish Persephone,
She spends the dark months
        struggling towards us
                with her light held up
Like a Christmas Tree, light-bursting.
        She is away, or so it seems
                during the New Year –
In March and most of April too
        she is struggling towards us
                through the mineral mire,

And through the oiled lakes underground
        and through the cities of ore
                more capacious far
Than the small towns of our Duchy;
        our underworld is a Birmingham of rocks
            through which she toils
Emerging at a mine-tip in flowers
        on Goonhillie, St Day,
            and as she rises it is like
An electricity you see because you feel it;
        When she is with us
            people live in sunlight
As the blessed do visible and invisible too
        for the seven other months –
            all trees shake their presence out:
Leaving her consort in the living rock,
        she rises learned
            from her imprisonment.

DAZZLE

A house in the North,
            on the opposing shore,
                        a home, like mine,
Voyaging through the night,
            a house black as a cat;
                        then the sun rose to the right,
The windows shone like gongs,
            she stepped out
                        on to her patio,
Clad in yellow silk.
            How had she stepped out in yellow
                        through the gold of the windows?
It was a chymical problem
            and a topological one;
                        where she had come from, walking
On the patio, smelling like the sun
            in her curcubite
                        of yellow silk?
I saw from the further shore
            how her windows
                        flashed the sun
As she opened them
            over the broads as far
                        as to my window,
Dazzling me with light-flux
            in which she appeared.
                        But how, then,
In that flexing beam of silk
            could I have smelt her robe
                        and felt her touch
On my arm for she has entered
            this room across the water.

OLD SUNSHINE

He called to his fencing-master
   to execute the boy;
      there was a bright strong light
Running down the blade
   in anticipation of its drink;
      the martial maestro paused
Though hesitation was death;
   more than once
      had watched the boy stop
At the seventh tree in the wood,
   the one whose fruit
      left a shuddering taste in the mouth,
The Old Sunshine or laburnum
   that enchanted the copse with lingering poison.
      So he whispered to his Prince
That the boy was intoxicated
   with the seeds of Old Sunshine
      and therefore by the law of the land
Could not be killed in that pre-mortem condition;
   the boy would be confined
      into prison for as long as it took
His royal accuser to die;
   someone would be found
      to smuggle him supplies
Of Old Sunshine,
   whose light would maintain him
      in his enchanted condition, sunshine
Taking care of her own.

MISTRESS-ORGANIST

The women in boxy
      white hats
            having rented the most
Expensive pews
      chatter about sorcery
            but are silenced
By the shiver of the organ,
      a lady fellow-devil
            dances on the keys
In brilliant pumps;
      they all grin mutually like keyboards.
            In her charcoal-grey suit
Like a graphite star
      the Mistress-organist comes
            grinning like a keyboard.
She had to have me in the organ-loft
      above the choir where the wooden flues
            of profound notes were fastened
To their lung-machine
      like upright coffins
            buzzing to the Last Trump,
And the sixteen-foot burdoun shook
      our truckle-bed down the oblong room:
            'Did it move for you . . . ?'
How the boy-soprano
      trilled out as we came!
            and in the Monk's Pond
Fish like treasure rose
      in silver ingots
            to the sudden rain.
Now she discusses her concert
      in this privacy
            with her conductor, me,

We are unperturbed
      by the long trail
            of vagina-juice
That tapers over the sheet
      in the displaced truckle-bed
            lying open like the world's book,
Like the score of the world (like valuta
      the fish rise
            pouting at the rain).

MASS

I saw a moon held up.
        The wheat was a two-sexed Eucharist.
        The crossing for me
Was by true Moon.
        My father jauntily disordered.
           Pete holds his hand tightly
In the grand village of death.
        Raw waters emerging from their shells.
        A double dawn
Caused by a solar eclipse at sunrise.
        The waves of the shell,
          the shawls of the seer.
After shells, ships:
        SS Flax, Silverlid, Trigonia, Cardium,
          Clan, Torocas, Cyrona, Pinna,
Trombey, Burm, their wakes
        pass into the chalk of shells.

THE RAINBOW

The great reservoir
        hangs up inside itself;
                it reflects a sky
Corroded like zinc,
        in its pewter-coloured surface
                a small squall
Patches the water
        into roughened metal:
                you shall perceive
All the colours of the world
        in the cold gust crossing:
                to sip
At a tumbler of its water is
        to set open a glass of dream.
                A clew of sunbeams hangs
Suddenly in the brimming glass,
        sipping this water at her lips
                charged her
With its reflections,
        moistened her yoni
                with nude water,
And she felt a rainbow
        of pleasure
                shining through the squall
Within her,
        up there,
                and in her reservoir.

STUDENT BEDSIT

The cold windows
        run with dew, black mould
                is sketching a great eye
Over their bed,
        a cracked window
                leaks a map of Ireland,
But she has been out
        in the sun buying cabbages
                in the sunny air
And as she spoke
        I smelt the fresh
                landscape from her lungs
As though the beautiful day
        had been photographed in its perfume
                and now she breathed it out,
Lighting the bedroom
        of fading posters and graffiti;
                and at other times she brings
The cool clear stars from the sky
        into the twilit early morning room;
                bacon and eggs
Are consumed
        indoors under the starry sky.

VISION OF DUESSA

I saw Duessa when I was young,
    too young for the laboratory of her perfumes
      to deceive me with
Her ordinary masks and glamours; in that alchemy
    she was a remote
      and glorious figure,
Or a close and glorious figure,
    but I knew what was
      underneath that alchemy
And odour; I saw
    the Duessa-nature early, and it was
      loving-kindly.
She wished a kiss, the crone did,
    and like a hot poker plunged
      in a spicy drink
Clouds of agreeable influence
    rose about her
      and changed her features,
Even her voice-tone.
    How beautiful she is,
      how beautiful!
Cry all the men in love;
    but I know
      she was better than beautiful;
She was magic.
    It was my privilege in my childhood latency
      to see her clothe
And unclothe herself
    in these garments and wardrobe machineries
      of fascination;
She was a perfect nudity almost lost
    among the swinging vanities
      I entered for my kiss.

Recent research has uncovered a 'grannie perfume' pheromone that gives elderly
people a caring atmosphere (*New Scientist*, 3 July 1999).

LECHERIES

I

Adam and Eve clothed themselves
     in the slough of the serpent, which
          was silk, spun by a worm.
Observe the lechery of the infant wriggling
     at the breast, hence this word:
          Leche, milk.
The words would not survive
     without their darker meanings: *Lych*,
          the snake-porch of the ancestor-dead
Demanding rebirth.

II

When a woman desires a child she installs
     not only an egg in her well
          but also a serpent, swimming.
These are skin-changing forces –
     weather, Moon, and woman in their courses –
          that change you into
This sloughing weresnake, attendant serpent.
     My snake makes entry and discovers
          a cavern full of fellow-snakes,
The snakes awake.
     Custodians of the serpent
          paint themselves and draw
On their faces new faces; it is
     their auto-suggestion to themselves:
          'It's fine today,
I will feel as fine
     as I look!' and paint themselves as one
          might dedicate a temple to the snakes

Which are drawn out
        by sweetly-odorous precincts.
                Look! she bares herself to the waist
And raises two serpent-handfuls;
        why should a snake smell of honeycomb?
            It does.
The wax breaks softly as I enter,
        the honey flows:
                food for the snakes,
Ourselves, and plenty over.

TRIAL BY MALLET

He was lean, fast-moving,
        darkly-handsome,
                wore white-and-black
Like me; I had to fight
        this younger man
                in the long and arch-roofed room
Like a storm-drain, ancient brick
        scrawled over
                with white lime crusts
And hedgehogged with pencil-stalactites.
        It was raining solid rods,
                water-curtains muffled
The entrance-arch, inside
        the shelly pendules started
                to drip clear water.
A third man in formal dress was present,
        he carried, for the *coup de grâce*,
                a lunar penknife blade,
Its small scythe flashing
        in the ambiguous light
                of two torches
Struck flaming in iron brackets.
        We each grasped
                the thick stems
Of the iron-bound mallets;
        it was Trial by Mallet, I could see us
                as we would be
If this duel began,
        crushed bone creaming
                in the black cloth it rent,
Two men moused by the cats-clawed mallets.
        One of us demanded
                a limit on the tally

Of blows, our umpire
                  grinned like that cat
                              and shook his head,
We could almost see the pleased tail swish
                  under his tailcoat;
                              this shared glimpse
Made me remember
                  that my opponent was also my friend,
                              near to a brother,
By trade a pilot
                  full of strategies, vitality, navigations,
                              so why did we plan to fight
In this storm-drain underground,
                  whose body was to be flushed
                              out to sea on the flood?
My friend, I thought,
                  the storm is coming on, with thunder, soon
                              we shall be fighting
Knee-deep in its torrents.
                  I caught his eye, and as one man
                              we turned towards the umpire
For answers, the mallets heavy
                  as our children's heads.

HA!

The plum horse
   with the tears of gum
      dried on the velvet muzzle,
The tears that fly in the race, in the gallop
    they are the rain of the horse,
       its rainbow in the mane
Passes into true horse-nature Ha!
     It runs in the rainshadow of the wind,
       rainbow and sweatbow,
The horse leaps into the breeze,
    it leaps into the distance,
      its knobbly whinny
Knotty as its plaited mane,
    the croissant of its mane,
      the horse turning
Into baps
    in the oven of its blood:
      his balsam tears,
The buttery muzzle,
    his thunderhead mane,
      the lightning of his whinny,
His thunder-hewed flanks.

TRUE WASP

On the twentieth of this November
        I noticed wasps
                eating a toad flattened by cars –
They were tearing away
        strips of toad-skin
                braided to the asphalt;
Later the same day I saw
        a dead mouse opened by its own gas
                with wasps studding its backbone:
It was their season,
        turning horror to vigour;
                turning eyes downwards
I saw wasps pinching
        fine ginger crumbs
                from a reclining dogturd;
By the sweet hum of the small power-station
        I was caught in our mother the rain
                and still the wasps came weaving
Between the drops slow as syrup,
        never struck and always steady,
                entering the machinery
To collect light from the cables,
        winged vessels distilling sharp venom
                in the great wasp
Nesting hum of the transformers
        painted yellow and black, separating
                bitterness from light.

A MIDWIFE

She brought light to the eyes
        of the newborn in darkness;
                she brought her candle
To the childbed in the shuttered room
        with the darned sheets.
                Mother and child
Appeared like cinema
        thrown on those sheets, wavering
                with their uncertain breath;
She brought in her fluttering candle,
        and red wine for the mother
                to drink, to pass
Hints of spirit to the newborn;
        liquor thereafter stood for light.
                He drinks now
His glass of wine raised to his midwife
        and the liquor risen
                from the death of grapes
Is her teat waking him
        from the black veil, shining.

CORE

We cannot hear the voice
   of this machine,
      they scan the unborn
With ultra-sound —
    Will the foetus not be bonded
      to this song,
Will inaudible whistles not
    become its mother?
       Is whistling at girls
With ultra-sound not wrong?
    A transparent window opens
      suddenly in their bellies
Disclosing a buddha-face
    in shadows on a VDU
      semaphoring its arms
Below the belt:
    through the swiftly-transparent
      muscle-skin walls
A sudden clear glass appears
    and suspended there
      the star
Of fivepoints shines
    within the apple-womb
      weaving her fingers,
Beating at her temple walls:
    the Core;
      or, the sixpointed male
Waving to us
    through the skin and flesh.

UNDERNEATH THE ARCHES

The arch remains
        standing but only because
                all the stones strive
To collapse at the same time;
        there is a salty equivocal chorus
                singing within
The strained stones
        that fall and stand at once.
                The noble-nosed cat
Lurks within the arch
        like an eagle come to earth
                who folded his wings
Forever and will fly no more.
        There is no spirit without its echo
                such as the twilight
Of the arch and the cat's blackness
        and its stretch
                which seems to reach
The very dome of the arch.
        Enter the spinster
                who drags her wooden chair
Into the cool shade of the arch's stones
        and who feeds a cloud of wool
                into her spindle,
Into the art of the point
        at which a mass becomes a thread;
                rain stipples the dust
Which is dry as wool
        where she spins with her cat
                at her feet, and as the cloud

Condenses into threads
        of our drinking-water,
                simultaneously she spins
A woollen shirt for my father's back.

THE OTHER CARGO

The rays of the moon
        are sweet and salty,
            the docks worked by
Every kind of ship,
        cargoes of tamarind,
            or sea-slugs,
Or stags' horns,
        and with every one
            the second, secret cargo;
Venture down
        into the aquarium hold whose walls are clear,
            you see the whole sea
Swimming towards you:
        this is the second cargo;
            meanwhile, on the docks
The silvery pilchards
        are laid in tall round barrels
            by the Fish Maidens who arrange
The tails at the centre to create
        an inverse star
            pulled clean out of the ocean.

BENEVOLENCE

The moon wrestles with the sky,
        with the white blood,
                with the semen.
Is he hurt? No, he is dead.
        I liked my own
                sweet afternoon in bed.
What a child came from their hobbies!
        She lifts the cat from the sofa
                like a sleeping-bag of black silk
In which a vagrant snores.
        The trees —
                the great birdsong engines —
Carry their weight lightly,
        and their song
                spreads over the county.
I dial my dentist —
        I hear birdsong
                over the handset. Outside
A line of birds grips hard
        the telephone wire and sings here too that
                birdsong is one of the beatitudes;
Let the cat
        sleep off his benevolence.

NOCTURNAL EMISSION

As I touch
   the fixed star of her clitoris
     her body gives off a potion of scents
Like a herb-bed in a sudden shower.
   Together, we set the rose in motion.
    There is
A strange shining taste in the air. Now
   it recurs everywhere.
     As she left us
The tension from the thundercloud
   lessened. We lifted our glasses
    and took a drink
Of thunderwater, we seemed
   less like people
     than garlands billowing
With their perfume in the instant
   before the rain fell.
    Now the women
Had all become giantesses, having added
   their invisible stature;
    the visible figure
Merely the nether part of a cresting
   thunderclap. They had become trees
    and transpired the weather
In clouds above as trees do
   by their emissions. There was
     an arresting fragrance from the moon
Passing through her zodiac
   which is her grove;
    we had set the rose in motion;

The young queen stood singing
                dressed in gilded robes
                            in the rain
Drenched in her self-emission.

DREAM VISITOR

Honey poured on silk: synaesthetic space;
        her chant kept breaking up
                into the shrieks of gulls;
I slept through the storm,
        and half-waking
                I heard it as a psalm.
In these stormy days rings are tight.
        I wiped the tears from her face
            with a silk square;
These tears were tacky
        with the electricity of the storm,
                her silk dress crackled
As if starched; her tears
        cohered, like honey on silk;
                crepitating, she moved like trees:
When we kissed,
        the sparkle chapped our lips,
            the current passed, the silks
Clung as if drenched.

CARABUS VIOLACEUS

The violet ground beetle
        full of luminous cockaigne;
                the solid wooden words:
The trees carry up
        their invisible writing
                that becomes clouds;
Along the willow-path
        small clouds
                linger in the tree-heads
Like ghosts sitting
        in the trees which are
                the anatomy
And physiology of the ghosts;
        (the spermbright bees . . .)
                The sea reaches far
Into the land,
        you are never without its sound of ghost
                heard not just with the ears:
The spirit-movement of ghost;
        the greenbeard wildman
                in his chair of blossom,
They seek him out, the spermbright
        spiritual bees, the hives
                smoke dry water
That is ghost,
        that is sweet sweet
                ghost.

AUTUMN LOVELETTER

The skin-of-the-earth-shining
   as you walk towards the tree
     which has exuded
A sheening envelope of sap;
   it is like a door
     opened in the trunk
And, inside the door,
   something to drink.
     I move closer, and think,
After Bunyan:
   'In this Land the Shining Ones
     commonly walked,
Because it was
   on the borders of heaven.' The aroma
     and the fragrance of new thoughts
Were perceptible in these designs
   of balsams and barks . . .
     What is a Grail-Winner?
Why, any man who frees the waters
   in the woman by her consent, which means
     he is a rainmaker
As she is. He knows
   from a bad temper in the sky
     that the rain will soon
Come down here: irritability
   above the barley-fields
     seldom persists, it relents
In heavy and opulent showers. The barley-beard
   pierces every drop that falls . . .
     A bird fighting its shadow
On a whitewashed wall,
   coming at it
     with beating wings, stabbing

Beak and claws . . .
        that apple-tree's fruit
                with stars in its mansion
Shall serve as meat for all;
        the thrush energetically
                excavating the last ones
In the tree,
        taking boxer's stance on the apple-domes
                and stabbing into them
With swift wet strokes . . .
        at Maenporth the woman
                climbs out of the plasm,
Out of the darkened tabernacles,
        and there is
                the golden-glow
Of the heroic skin, alive
        with its inexcusable hazard. She
                drops her soiled robes
As she comes, the black
        off the golden glow,
                the mudworks full
Of emergency eyes
        that marvel at her form . . .
                the nectar of the tree
Is flowing from the doorway
        under the shining lintel:
                any tree, mound,
Standing stone
        can take you thus inside, if you have
                freed the water, the nectar.
Now the pelvic cups tilt and kiss
        and are of the same pulse. We see
                the various flowers
And flower-gardens we are made of
        inside – the carnation
                of the heart,

The daffodil banks
        of the spleen,
                the jasmine kidney. We watch
Free cities of flowing nectar;
        all the citizens in polished carapace
            feast at its banks:
This is the start
        of Unbottle, or Autumn,
            when the pleasure
Of smells
      is at its most
           perilous.

SENIOR LOVE

An oak is love,
                senior love.
                                The thunder-canopies glide
Above the forest hills they darken,
                thundershadow laid upon deepening
                                thundershade, and the wind
Rising.
                After the storm,
                                walking in the air of love
Through the crocodilian boles
                pillared further
                                than one can see,
Wooden walls
                through which one may pass
                                as a ghost passes
To the sound of gentle thunder,
                your silent scent parting,
                                every leaf thundering a little.
Oaks are a winged being,
                like Eros, who shows his genitals
                                as oaks do; in the thunder
With the lightning streaming
                across every leaf, the oaks
                                wave their million-leaved boughs
And expose their flowers
                out of which, travelling
                                further than sight
Pours the air of love.

THE HARPER

Shiny waterbeetles
           scribe the pond, each one
                      the centre of its circular signature,
Each one the centre
           of its circular harp;
                      these harps collide
Sending out graven improvisations,
           sketches, line-drawings
                      and scrawling signatures,
All the same signature,
           never identical,
                      now an ellipse,
An egg drawn on water, a one system
           with two beetle-centres . . .
                      the woman swimming
At the heart of her harp,
           swimming in her evening clothes
                      that make fresh signatures,
Entering the music like Ophelia
           but a strong swimmer,
                      in her presence
The music bends,
           turning over and over
                      in its helicals,
Her orchestra skirt and blouse
           winding conches and sails;
                      how the cloth clings
In a lover's chord . . .
           Her love is the fresh
                      and talkative spring she
Couples with,
           and in it layers herself,
                      clothes scribing out

The depths of the river . . .
        the woman swimming looks up
                and the whole woodland pond
Is reflected in her eyes,
        her hair twining and searching
            in the signature:
Woman harpist clothed in the forest brook.

PRESENT FROM CHERNOBYL

They esteemed the wasting sickness
        and its rales, their mountain
                glows at night –
It is the radioactive treasure
        of those latterday Incas,
                their Eldorado
Is chalky, phosphorescent,
        the glow of morning clouds,
                the pearl-shine,
The zinc light of those
        high treasure-ships
                voyaging from Chernobyl
Full of bones that shine in the dark
        like a child's Halloween spook,
                which is why we gave them
Such toys, to worship the skull that is to come
        shining like a far-off star approaching, with
                the crack in the chest,
The ancient rales,
        the old lump,
                the lung's strepitus, the catch
In the breath that may everlast.
        I heard the rales
                crackling in my father's chest,
The visitor of eighty, with his hand-bones
        like a present done up
                in ribbons of blue
And fading scarlet.

LONG-BODIED SHADOW

The cat relishes
   every corner of the house,
      couchant on discarded jerseys,
Clawing hats down,
   sleeping on them, call him
      Hatcat; he clawed out from
The linen cupboard
   the long-johns of yellowed cotton
      the exact colour
Of their owner's death-face,
   the yellow-white
      that dissectors used to get
Under their fingernails,
   death had got in an odorous colour
      in these long pants!

Greatly daring I lifted them to smell –
   Palmolive, pure, but
      I needed badly at once to burn them,
Once I deliberately smelt
   as an act of friendship
      reaching down through the grave
The armpit of my dead friend's overcoat,
   it was very ripe
      with his approaching death
Spent in the pub, I heaved
   and passed out.
      Once he and I were walking
A country road after closing-time,
   we had plenty to drink with us
      in cans, the fizz of the beer

And the fizz of the small flowers
                on the boughs was all the same
                                fizz, he said –
He wanted to lie in the long grass and piss
                straight up into the air
                                like a flowering tree,
Like an ancestor,
                which is what he does
                                among the other stones.
The cat enjoys the house,
                its roofs and voids
                                like a long-bodied shadow
Of those times:
                the same fizz,
                                of a darker colour.

THOROUGHFARE

He drives in silence,
        he likes to hear
                the sound of England passing
Underneath his car,
        a mile on mile windscreened
                shadow-theatre,
Carving out his headlighted way;
        he has read about
                the first photo-writing
On silver-sensitised leather
        like printing on somebody's skin;
                that's what he's got –
A sensitised skin which takes
        silver photos of the night.
                He agrees he likes
Driving at high noon –
        but it is his lower soul
                that loves to hear
The imprinting of his tyres on the road
        and the passing of the earth beneath:
                mile upon mile
On roads of skin at night, at night.

DAWN

They squeaked,
            pulling at his arms
                        'More sex, more sex!'
But he embraced only
            a girl called Dawn.
                        And long after the sun had risen
He went on embracing her
            in the twilit hangars
                        of the great forests,
And through the night waited
            in the great cathedral
                        for the East window
To tincture with Dawn;
            noisy and oblivious
                        the others took Mass
Like five hundred lovers
            in one large bedroom.

WILD CRY FROM THE
GLITTERING PHARMACY

She will mount on the back
       of a raincloud
              followed from the window,
The tree will be the nurse
       of the dew and the rain,
              the evergreen
Dripping like a wet-nurse,
       the glittering pharmacy
              of the big sleep, the halls
Of mirrors and potions
       in the magnetic sleep at dawn
              after your sexual calls
Like a stretching tree;
       the open doors of the pharmacy
              like bonfires of flowers.
All the stars look bland
       and begin to fade
              as if the medicine had purged them,
Or unscrambled them during your cries,
       for you kept to the vantage point
              you found where the tree of dawn
Drops liquid fruit, rattles its leaves.

SWEETHEART SIESTA

Great white and gold
        cruise liners, the shipyards folded
                in a navy of seagulls
And bright, fiery, clever sailors;
        stroking the ship's cat
                I detect a certain
Dangerous tone
        in his warm black fire;
                he patrols, pacing out
His own invisible shipyard
        that builds itself
                in the warm South wind,
Windows and paving opening in the wet heat,
        piss-building its towers
                in the shadowy corners:
There is a big sleep
        coming off this South wind,
                and I am late
For work, my sleepyhead
        like a nautilus shell
                full of the calls and sails
Of sailors and the golden drone
        of cruisers and the cat's touch
                perfumed like a ship of sweethearts.

PIANISM

Fluid pianism. It was as if
      he sat down at a waterfall, it flowed
            over his fingers and they wrestled
With the disappearing water; the piano's
      frame and strings reappeared
            from moment to moment in the busy
                  water
Then disappeared in a sudsy flux of brilliant
      current, or were marked across by some
            new breeze of tributary torrent but
The sheerwhite style was creaselessly present:
      something in the speed; his hair flowed too
            down to his shoulders and was a part
Of the music seen as well as heard,
      its sound matched the brilliance
            of his hair-gloss and the white foam
Flowed over the piano's terraced ledges
      down his legs and over the stage
            into the audience soaking them with Liszt.

HORMONE HARVEST

A metal liberated
        and dissolved in the air,
                a leaking scent
By whose means, say,
        Jupiter grazes the earth
                and great events
Mount skywards; equally, a bowl
        of earth from the garden
                emits its secrets
Of that apparently humble
        yet unknown substance, its
                crumbly slither-touch
And its rabid perfume;
        and the companionship
                of the working river,
Of the gliding soil, living all his life
        by the river and its soil,
                in companionship with glassworks, by
A partnership of power-stations and bungalows,
        and the female sex-hormone
                grafted into the water –
Nipping the pill out of its calendar smartcard,
        urinated into the rivers
                and making us all women:
The river smiles, a charged-up woman,
        yet that is not such a new thing
                as the forests have been sending down
Their hormone-harvest since all began.

METAL BLOOM

A thick shift
   of gossamer has fallen across
      the ploughed field like
Spun tin: the furrows are clothed
   in loose silk
      with a sheen bending on it
Like a lake in the sun, a bright path
   watering
      across the silk field;
Nearby, a little cliff of red stone
   in which wasps build mansions
      of stone dust and paper;
Myself at home in the mason's yard
   where the quarried stones are piled
      in their henges, and
Bees visit a tin pail silvery as birches,
   the pail sounding their tune
      like branched birches:
A galvanised bloom
   the bees visit drinking.

NOSTALGIA LOCALE

The heat came off her skin
        like a tar road in August; she was
            shack-sassy,
There was abrasion in our love;
        but the gifted stranger came
            offering gifts
Out of a majolica humidor,
        laughing at our surprise and gratitude
            at the grass cigars,
Marijuana coronas. We all lit up, he began
        to play the bottleneck
            like an angel, the throat
Of his white shirt
        sliced open like a wedding-cake
            on his rich-fruit skin
And he looked good enough to eat
        as he smoked, grinning. I thought
            as I puffed my weed,
This is the way Wisdom changed hands
        among the wise, by gifts,
            and she and I are so poor
We feel no obligation to our angel;
        but will she be sassy
            after he has gone, the gifts
All smoked, or welcome me more thoroughly
        into her August heat . . . ?

WHO DOETH WONDROUS THINGS

Lightning-struck wood is soft
            and easily-worked.
                        Struck rosewood.
Struck cedar. She took something
            out of my aching back, and washed
                        her hands of it.
I smelt the colognes
            of her period
                        on her face and neck.
The knot-garden peered
            over her shoulder,
                        A thousand million skeletons
All interlocked in the earth.
            The Goddess is reputed to be
                a wonderful reaper:
She carries, that is,
            the Moon's sickle.
                      La Bois de la Lune,
Needs no roof but the sky:
            they tear open the temple's
                high thatch
For the dead to fly easily,
            plucked up into the full Moon
                      which is her arena,
In the flood,
         in the tide-hiss
                of its silversand floor.

WITCH CIRCLE

The white shadows
           of elder spirits dancing:
                     rusty hulls, docked;
I had committed a sexual working
           with a rubber dolly
                     that came folded up
Through the post, but this too
           was a symbol of her Goddess,
                     even this, this pelt, this shell;
She was sorry for me, so she showed me
           her little aroma or ghost
                     or guardian, the moon
Having been drawn down upon her
           into the Circle and then
                     into the astral, the chemicals
At her fingertips and in her breath,
           my ears twitching like a cat's
                     to the black sounds
Of her quiet chanting;
           deep underground
                     the flickering candlelight
Of the worshippers there
           shines upwards and we pace safely,
                     Aethyr in the influence
Of the orchards all around,
           out of the applewood, the castle
                     where the tree lives,
The smell of potent
           spirit on our breath
                     when we had taken
No alcohol.

WINDS

Air-fountains and airfalls;
        the ocean is the quick queen
                turning back on herself.
A cold and crusty gale;
        hurricane comes from a Taino word,
                'Hurican', or Evil Spirit;
The cool Pontias
        from the Rhône gorges – then
                the darkness that can be felt
Of the Khamsin, which is
        the ninth plague of Egypt;
                the wind pours seaward now;
Twilight, the time of changing worlds;
        I felt myself invincibly at one with her
                as though she
Had turned the weather –
        which she might have done, merely
                to eat our calm supper together;
It was the kind of fascination
        an abyss of winds can cause
                drawing a person
Very near the edge, to the very edge.

From her small notebook: series 2, no. 1 . . .
        . . . returned home for our skinsleep
                of great beauty in which
Broad soft vapours came off our bodies,
        to the closed eyes a brightly-lit
                gourmet restaurant;
We fed impalpably on those same rare vapours,
        a banquet
                of spiritual milk,

A balsamic bill of fare;
It is a land wind, seaward,
at that soft time in the evening.
All the plants, like ourselves, are
giving up their balsams
and fertilising the sea with them,
Unlearned, plentiful.

THEME-DREAM

Touching my tongue
        to her hole, there was
                an electrical jolt
Like the stud
        of a powerful torch battery,
                the kind that goes on
For ever; then there was an electrical theme-park
        seen through the skin
                full of invisible but melodious
Carousels; ferris wheels and booths of chance,
        and this was a dream clothed by
                the actual visit
We had made that afternoon.
        The children ran ahead
                between the model buildings
One-tenth the size, there was Pisa leaning
        and the munificent Swiss chalet
                full of accordion mirth
On self-changing records ever-lasting
        to which the girls were dancing
                before the David
Of Michaelangelo
        like a golden calf;
                they danced with joy
Because of his neat genitals
        like a draw-string shammy bag
                with a weasel peering from it:
The two were only nine at that time,
        this the only wedding-muscle they'd seen,
                so sweet and neat they danced
And then the voice above of splitting-open drowned
        the Switzer jollification, and the axe
                of thunder sang in the black

Cloud towers, the snaking blue fire
                played about the shammy-bag
                              of valiant David
In the pouring rain.

PAINTING THE SHIPS

The florid smells
        as they paint the steel decks
                in the colours of flowers,
Readying the steel flowers
        to float off to tropical islands
                of flowers, floating
Scenery of the invisible isles.
        The men in colourful hard hats
                do it, small flowers
Painting the great flower,
        pollinating it with colours
                and turpentine
Which flies away on the local breezes.
        It is Falmouth in Bloom in the docks
                and parks. The ship
Floating in like a huge, grand old building
        that had not been lived in
                for many years.
Building in bloom, afloat.
        Clattering with resonant tools
                as in repairing an engulfing bell.
The handler's voice
        sings a handler's song
                which echoes through the cabins,
Decks, holds, funnels and bulkheads.
        The power of song and its echoes
                bloom to the eyes, the whistling
As of one worker in the immense apartments.

ORCHARD END II

In the rainshower
        under the green skirts,
                sheltering with my mother;
Beneath the oak
        the sudden magistery
                of the oak smell,
The oak coming forth
        with a hiss in the leaves,
                as the oak comes
Into the rainfall
        the ground darkening
                and then puddling with mirrors,
Stepping out into the world of the oak,
        into the world changed
                by the oak-elixir, charged,
The rain lowers herself on the oak
        and the oak comes
                into the rain
By the house called Orchard End,
        either because it was the end
                of the great orchard of Malden,
Or the end of paradise
        that was expected to fade
                as one grew up,
But it didn't
        because of the oak coming forth
                under my mother's shade
Which has since
        become the oak-shade.

IN PARTHENON BEATAE
MARIAE ET SANCTAE COLUMBAE
ET AGATHAE

I

In the Virginhouse of Blessed Marys and Holy Doves
And Kindly Ones they grind pigment for their faces
For in response to changing weathers, seasons,
New styles of countenance are manufactured;
Successive seasons of the year are marked
For solidarity so they may manifest like one
Communicating spirit: each New Moon they gouge
Dark sockets with their collyrium and all of them
Menstruate together with their hollow eyes
And wear no perfume but their natural opiates
And most men are affronted by these declarations
Though in full moon mating-times they fall hard for
The arching surprised eyebrow-pencil and the faint
Gold skins, and the searchlight directed up
From the bosom and throat by the lily-blouses
With their gold pollen of a face; and thus
An image from the calendar steps into our bed.

II

She opens the bathroom door to me
In her white mud-mask which looks
As though her skin has turned to bone

Which gives me a real turn, as if she communed
Inwardly with that divinity whose mask is clay;
'Try it, Peter; in it you look like Death –
Death that washes off skin as smooth as a child's.'

LAST POEM

(transcribed from Peter's handwritten draft)

Buzz-saw cry of the gannet,
a ghost of water,

his outside child

The next station is God
Mind the doors!

Alive in those shadow-streets